BE A POWERHOUSE FOR GOD

CLAIRE ELIZABETH GROSE

Copyright © 2025 by Claire Elizabeth Grose

Compiled and edited by Michael Grose and June Kennedy

All rights reserved. No portion of this publication may be reproduced, stored in a retrieval system or transmitted in any form by any means – electronic, mechanical, photocopying, recording, or any other –except for brief quotation in printed reviews, without the prior written permission of the publisher.

Unless indicated otherwise, all scripture quotations in this book are from the following source:

The Good News Bible: The Bible in Today's English Version (TEV) © 1976 by the American Bible Society. Used with permission.

ISBN 978-0-6459888-3-3

Author contact information - clairegrose.heartmatters@gmail.com

Version 1.0

DEDICATION

This book is dedicated to Lailah Rose,
My beloved Granddaughter

CONTENTS

DEDICATION	IV
CONTENTS	V
PREFACE	VIII
ACKNOWLEDGEMENTS	X
PART ONE	1
MY DAILY PRAYER	4
KEEP YOUR LIGHT BURNING	5
WRAPPED IN LOVE	6
LIVE GOD EVERYDAY	7
THE BLESSINGS YOU PASS MY WAY	8
SEEK HIS FAVOUR	9
NO CARE TOO SMALL	10
OVERFLOWING BLESSINGS	11
KEEP FAVOUR WITH GOD	14
A TIMELY REWARD	15
KNOW HIM AS A BROTHER	16
I TRULY KNOW HIS LOVE	17
HE WILL SPUR YOU ON	18
CALL HIS BLESSINGS	19
GOD IS LOVE	20
GOD'S POWER MOMENTS	21
OVERFLOWING PEACE	22
CLAIM GOD'S BLESSING	23
BLESSINGS IN HIS WORD	26
BEAUTIFUL BEYOND WORDS	27
PRECIOUS IN HIS EYES	28
WALKING IN HIS LIGHT	29
PART TWO	30
POWER ME	33
KEEP REVERENCE FOR GOD	34
THE FAITHFUL	35
THE SELF IN ME	36

RISE ABOVE THESE DOUBTS	37
REST IN HIS LOVE	38
YOU KNOW AND YOU SEE	41
IN HIS NAME	42
PASSAGE OF LIFE	43
OPEN HEARTS	44
MATURITY IN FAITH	45
LIFETIME FRIENDS	46
YOU KNOW ME	49
KINDLY DEEDS	50
KEEP PEACE IN YOUR HEART	51
I'M WAITING ON YOU LORD	52
I'M IN YOUR HANDS	53
EVERYTHING IN ITS PLACE	54
CONSENT TO HIS LOVE	57
COME AS YOU ARE	58
PATIENCE	59
CLEAR IT AWAY	60
CHALLENGES	61
BEFRIEND THE SAVIOUR	62
YOU WILL GROW IN HIS LOVE	63
BAPTISM OF HOLY LOVE	64
THE PRECIOUS NAZARENE	65
THE CHRISTIAN HEART	66
TALK THROUGH YOUR HEART	67
STAY CONNECTED	68
PART THREE	**69**
THE ME I THOUGHT I KNEW	72
HIS LOVE WILL PREVAIL	73
REACHING INTO ETERNITY	74
PROCLAIM YOUR TRUST AND FAITH	75
PLACE PRAYERS IN HIS HANDS	76
MY REAL HOME	77
RHAPSODY OF LOVE	80
REST IN HIS SPIRIT	81

AWAKENING	*82*
THE YOU I LOVE	*83*
YOU KNOW US WELL	*84*
STAND FIRM IN HIS LOVE	*85*
PART FOUR	86
CALVARY'S NAZARENE	*89*
BE AN EASTER LILY	*90*
IN PASSION AND POWER	*91*
HOLY WEEK	*94*
REUNION	*95*
HER NAME WAS MARY	*98*
HALLELUJAH IN THE HIGHEST	*99*
IN THE MANGER HE LAY	*100*
NO GIFTS UNDER THE TREE	*101*

PREFACE

Two things I just wanted to say about this book are, why I started writing and how I came by the title.

I grew up in the 1950's-1960's in Adelaide, South Australia, my life was pretty simple but wonderful. I was very lucky to have a secure family life, and my Mum and Dad brought the family up to treat others with respect, do the right thing, be courteous, and respect your elders. We had a strict upbringing and even as adults our parents never criticized us but encouraged us to do our best in life. They were "Aussie battlers" but we always managed to make it through the tough times!

They were people of integrity and cared about others and instilled that into our family.

Church was a big part of our lives growing up. We went to Sunday School at an early age and progressed up through the appropriate groups as we got older.

Youth groups, camps and church anniversaries were all important to the whole family. We competed in church sports teams, basketball and tennis with other parishes across Adelaide. Life-long friendships were in the making and cherished golden memories to look back on that would never fade.

Bible stories, hymns and choruses were all part of getting to know Jesus. This nurturing finally led me to the day Jesus came knocking on my heart's door. Being filled with the Holy Spirit is something I will never forget and the overwhelming power of His love that filled my whole being and propelled me to the front of the hall to give my heart to Him. No words can fully describe the joy I felt. That was in February 1968, I was 14 years of age. He has been my Shining Light ever since, and lives within me always.

So I thank my beautiful Mum and Dad for the way they raised me and for the foundation of knowing Jesus' love.

BE A POWERHOUSE FOR GOD

It was in His love that I started to write, in the Autumn of 1993. My journey has brought me to this book "Be a Powerhouse for God", my 13th book. In His Word He tells us to shine our light before others. "Your hearts and minds must be made completely new, and you must put on the new self, which is created in God's likeness and reveals itself in the true life that is upright and holy." Ephesians 4:23,24 - Good News Bible.

When we open our heart to receive Jesus, we also receive from God the gift of The Holy Spirit, who comes to live in our heart forever. He reveals God's ways to us and slowly changes the way we feel in our heart so we can be shining lights for Him.
"The Helper will come – the Spirit, who reveals the truth about God and who comes from the Father. I will send Him to you from the Father, and he will speak about me."
John 15:26 Good News Bible.

When I was a young Christian reading my Bible was really important to me in getting to know Jesus as my personal Saviour and became the foundation that I built my faith on.

It gave me strength and courage as I began life in the workforce at the age of 16. Coming from a sheltered upbringing it was my lifeline to self-confidence and adapting to social life at work.
The poems reflect the everyday feelings and emotions that we feel as we meet the challenges of life and how the great magnitude of God's love can help us rise above them.

Many of these writings have been my first words of whispered prayer, so much that I have been moved to write them down at once and continue on in His wonderful and absolute love.

Together we write as He provides my inspiration.

All glory to Him, my precious Lord Jesus!

ACKNOWLEDGEMENTS

My heartfelt thanks to my beloved family, my Mum and Dad, Lilly and Ken, and my siblings Jeanette, June, Carol, Gloria and Lynne, for their never ending encouragement and support to me. To the rest of the family, you are all a precious link that joins us together.

To Michael and Andrew for your continual support to me in fulfilling my passion of writing poems for the Lord to help others through His Word.

A huge thank you to Junie for editing my poems and the coffees and lunches we enjoyed along the way.

To Joy Furnell for her Crown of Thorns drawing, you have an amazing gift, thank you Joy.

A special thank you to Salisbury Uniting Church, Adelaide for photos. Used by permission.

A big thank you to Carol and Dennis, Jette and Pete, Lindsay, Michael and Andrea for great photos.

To my friends and Church Families, thank you for your love and support.

To my beautiful sons, Michael and Andrew, and your families. Thank you for loving me, and I am so glad He gave you to me. I cherish my grandchildren, I love you all so much.

To you the reader, thank you for picking this book up and I pray you will find His peace and love on the pages ahead.

May He shower you all with His love and blessings.

PART ONE

…"I am the light of the world," he said. "Whoever follows me will have the light of life, and will never walk in darkness."

John 8 : 12

HELP ME TO REFLECT…
YOUR SHINING LIGHT O'LORD…

"In the same way your light must shine before people, so that they will see the good things you do and praise your Father in heaven."

Matthew 5 : 16

MY DAILY PRAYER

Be with me, stay with me,
Close by my side,
Fill me with your peace and love,
So my spirit shall surely fly
To the heights in your love,
As only you can give,
Prepare me for this day ahead,
So in me you'll always live.

KEEP YOUR LIGHT BURNING

Keep your light burning
In the Saviour's love,
An endowment indeed
From God above.

He wants to see it shining
Every day of your life,
Especially on those shadows,
You can shine so bright.

He will power you ahead,
His supply never fails,
Keep your light burning
In His love you will prevail.

There is no other way,
Source it from the Lord,
Keep your light burning
With Holy Oil He will anoint.

Keep your light burning,
Others will surely see
The happiness inside you
Because you live for "Thee".

WRAPPED IN LOVE

You love us dearly Lord,
Your blessings are wrapped in love,
Stored in Your House
In the heavens above.

They come in different ways,
Sometimes we wonder why,
Who can explain?
Only God can supply!

He loves to reward us
For our faithfulness,
He longs for our attention
So us, He can truly bless.

God's blessings are wrapped in love,
A love that never ends,
They will prompt your heart to give
Through His Spirit that He sends.

LIVE GOD EVERYDAY

Live God everyday
For peace within,
Walk with the Master
He will show you how to live.

He knows your footsteps
And the path you will take,
So live God everyday
For His Names's sake.

He's there to comfort
If that's what you need,
He's there to celebrate
Your kindly deed.

Live God everyday
Because He loves you so,
Live God everyday,
He will never let you go.

THE BLESSINGS YOU PASS MY WAY

The blessings You pass my way Lord
I could never count,
I receive them every day,
That's what Your love's about.

From a smile to a friendly word
Or an act to lend a hand,
A word of encouragement
Are Your blessings, I understand.

The blessings You pass my way Lord
Can be large or small,
When I recognize them
I can appreciate them all.

The blessings You pass my way Lord
Might be near or far,
They will come from You
No matter where we are.

Keep my heart open
To receive them every day,
The splendour of Your love Lord
Are blessings You pass my way.

SEEK HIS FAVOUR

Seek the Lord's favour
In all you do,
Ask for daily guidance,
He has a plan for you.

He bestows special gifts
On each precious soul,
Each one different,
He longs for them to unfold.

There is no room for jealously
In His standards set,
Seek His favour
To help you be your best.

We compliment each other
By finding our special gift,
And using them to help others,
His favour we will win.

So, seek His favour always,
Go to Him for rest,
Seek His favour every day,
You, He will surely bless.

NO CARE TOO SMALL

A few words uttered in praise
To the Heavenly Father above,
He hears every word
When you open your heart.

No care is too small
For Him to understand,
Each one so precious
As He takes them in His hands.

Your plans may not come to light
As He rearranges your path,
Today's journey may be different
While He blesses your heart.

He craves your attention
For every detail of your life,
No care is too small
For Him to touch with His light.

Keep offering those whispers
To Him every day,
No care is too small
For Him to handle today!

OVERFLOWING BLESSINGS

Overflowing blessings
Are on their way to you,
When you know the Saviour
They will shine upon you.

They will come in many ways,
Some may be small or large,
Be sure they're heaven sent
Because you obeyed the Lord's commands.

Overflowing blessings
Are pure gold to me,
A favour I didn't see coming,
Was a blessing indeed.

Sometimes people in your life
Are a joy to see,
A friend to confide in
Who you can trust implicitly!

The Saviour sends His Spirit
To keep our light so bright,
Be sure to thank Him,
You are precious in His sight.

LORD…
YOU LIGHT MY PATH…

"The Lord is my light and my salvation…"

Psalm 27 : 1

KEEP FAVOUR WITH GOD

Keep favour with God
Because He knows your destiny,
Read His Word to know
How to live in reality.

Keep favour with God,
He knows the inner you,
Your thoughts and your heart,
The way you act and what you do.

Keep favour with God
To receive your heart's desire,
He wants us to obey Him,
That's what He requires.

Keep favour with God,
Enjoy the blessings He gives,
Accept His gift of salvation
Because for you He lives.

Keep favour with God,
Ask Him into your life,
You can live in His light forever
And receive the Crown of Life.

A TIMELY REWARD

Claim your reward today
To truly know His love,
Through your trust and faith
His measure will come.

They may be big or small
But no matter what they are,
You can be sure
They will be felt in your heart.

Each precious reward
Sent by God
Comes with His favour
For what you have done.

Even praying for someone
Who has a special need,
Will bring His reward
Because you are His precious seed.

KNOW HIM AS A BROTHER

Be yourself, talk to Him,
Know Him as a brother,
Confide your deepest cares in Him,
He's a friend like no other.

When a decision is pending
Take it to the Lord in prayer,
Know Him as a brother
Because He really cares.

When you need a helper,
If your spirit is low,
Know Him as a brother,
He will lift your cares, you know.

When you feel lonely,
With Jesus, spend some time,
Know Him as a brother,
No finer companion you will find.

Know Him as a brother,
No deeper love will flow,
A bond never broken
Because He loves you so.

Invite the King of Kings
Into your life today,
Know Him as a brother
His life for you He gave.

I TRULY KNOW HIS LOVE

I truly have to say
How I feel the Saviour's love,
Looking all around me
From the sea to the sky above.

His power so mighty
Moves my soul,
His precious Spirit within
Makes me whole.

The wonder of the sea,
How the ripples never stop,
The moon that shines so brightly
Above the mountain tops.

The glorious breeze
On an Autumn day,
The leaves changing to gold
As the green slowly fades.

These simple things
Take my heart away,
The power of God's love
I feel every day.

HE WILL SPUR YOU ON

When challenges arise
His love will spur you on,
Courage will be sent to you
To stand firm and strong.

Faith and trust are real,
A testament to the Lord,
His love will spur you on
To love Him even more.

You can depend
On His supply to build you up,
His love will spur you on
So you will always have enough.

He never sends more trials
Than you can solely bear,
His love will spur you on,
Your load with you He'll share.

His love will spur you on
When you use your trust and faith,
Through His Holy Spirit,
Your strength He will replace.

CALL HIS BLESSINGS

Call His blessings
Into your life today,
Each one is so special
Because it carried your name.

He wants you to be happy,
So call His blessings today,
You may not see them coming
But they are on their way.

Call His blessings today,
Some will shine like the stars,
But even little blessings
Can change who you are.

They are all made in heaven
From God's Holy hand,
Claim them as His gifts,
Some you may not understand.

He wants the best for you,
So claim His blessings now,
He will honour your trust
Thank Him with a bow.

GOD IS LOVE

God is love;
That's why I write,
My heart's desire
Is to help others see His light.

God is love;
Power and majesty,
He made all creation
Then He created you and me.

God is love;
In every way,
An anchor so real
You can talk to Him every day.

Take every care to Him,
Open your heart to His light,
God is love, eternal,
We are precious in His sight.

GOD'S POWER MOMENTS

Golden power moments are
God's glory shown to you,
It may be the perfume of a flower
Or a smile meant for you.

It may be a golden moment
When the Holy Spirit lays on your heart,
His peace in great magnitude
As He moves on your path.

God's power moments are
Crescent moon and stars at night,
Glorious changing sunsets
Will make your world so bright.

God's power moments arrive
In various shapes and forms,
Sent to thrill your heart
From our Saviour, Lord of Lords.

God's power moments
Sent through someone He wants to use,
His message sent from heaven
Because He loves you through and through!

OVERFLOWING PEACE

Some days the goodness in my soul
Overflows into my heart,
When I truly feel The Spirit
That's where it starts.

A feeling I can never ignore
It brings me inner peace,
I want to stay awhile
Because His love will never cease.

Overflowing peace will come,
A gift from the Lord
To all who will receive
His love that is for all.

You only have to ask
For this heavenly peace,
He will change you through His Spirit,
In His Name you will receive.

His overflowing peace
Will never let you down,
Call the Saviour today
He holds your Holy Crown.

CLAIM GOD'S BLESSING

Claim God's blessings today
And watch Him work in your life,
Rest on your trust and faith
That He will provide.

God's blessings will come,
Precious gifts He will lay on your path,
Some so unexpected,
Only God can surpass.

They will fill your heart with joy
That no words can explain,
Fears and doubts will fly away
Because God's blessings came today.

Your faith will be rewarded,
Claim God's blessings today,
You will see His awe and wonder,
His love will never fade.

YOUR GLORY LORD IS…
POWER AND MAJESTY…

"For the Spirit that God has given us does not make us timid; instead, his Spirit fills us with power, love, and self-control."

2 Timothy 1 : 7

BLESSINGS IN HIS WORD

There are blessings in His Word
That you can find on any page,
The guidelines for life
To help you through each stage.

As we grow through the years
And mature day by day,
Find His blessings in His Word,
They are there on any page.

You will find just what you need
If you want to relax,
Turn the pages of His Word,
Nothing you will lack.

His wisdom can be yours
When you turn to His Word,
His blessings will flow
Because you, He came to serve.

BEAUTIFUL BEYOND WORDS

Beautiful beyond words!
The measure of Your love Lord,
Fills my heart and soul
With Your Spirit's touch.

In the simple things around us
And in Your Holy Word
You are love itself
And You came to serve.

Beautiful beyond words,
The ebb of the sea,
Healing and soothing
I feel Your majesty.

Beautiful beyond words
Is the wonder of Your love,
Your precious Holy Spirit
Who brings You near to us.

PRECIOUS IN HIS EYES

Each one of us precious,
Precious in His eyes,
You made us all unique,
You we glorify.

Each one of us so different
But each with gifts to share,
God gave us special talents
For His glory so fair.

A light from within
To bless those around,
We are precious in His eyes
Where His love is found.

A kind act or friendly word
Is what He wants to see,
We are precious in His eyes
And part of His Family.

WALKING IN HIS LIGHT

Moments of pure joy
Are when you walk in His light,
When they come unexpected
They stand out in your mind.

Catching up with a friend
Over coffee, a treat,
Sharing special memories
Are days you just can't beat.

Blessings that shine
Are God's rewards for you,
It may be some kind word
Because you helped someone you knew.

Blessings that shine
Will come unexpectantly,
Walking in His light
You will want to help someone in need.

PART TWO

"I will praise your power, Lord God;
I will proclaim your goodness, yours alone."

Psalm 71 : 16

BE A POWERHOUSE FOR GOD

RECEIVE GOD'S BLESSINGS...
SO YOU CAN BLESS OTHERS...

"...your light must shine before people, so that
they will see the good things you do
and praise your Father in heaven."

Matthew 5 : 16

POWER ME

Power me in Your strength Lord
Every day of my life,
Enrich my spirit to Yours,
I'm precious in Your sight.

Power me in Your calm
As daily challenges arise,
Trusting I am in Your care,
That, I can't deny.

Power me in Your peace
That you gave me long ago,
The peace that comes from You,
On me You will bestow.

Power me in Your light
That will always shine,
Power me Lord forever,
You, my Lord Divine.

KEEP REVERENCE FOR GOD

Keep reverence for God
In all you do,
Though the world tells you different
Ask Him to help you.

Keep reverence for God
When decisions must be met,
Think of the outcome
With your heart and not your head.

Be solemn and still
In His Holy place,
Keep reverence for God
To praise His Holy Name.

Your rewards will be many,
Every day of your life,
Keep reverence for God
You are precious in His sight.

Keep reverence for God,
His heavenly hosts watch over you,
Read His Holy Word,
It will help you through.

You can be a powerhouse
When you keep reverence for God,
Through the Holy Spirit
You can lean upon.

THE FAITHFUL

The faithful to God
Will be rewarded in many ways
Because they listened to His voice,
They are committed to obey.

Though challenges will arise,
The faithful will trust in God,
Through the clamour of earths ways
They can overcome.

His light will go before them
Shining on their feet,
The faithful will keep moving
Though the path be slow and steep.

The faithful are His beloved
Because His Spirit spoke to them,
His joy and His rapture
He will always send to them.

THE SELF IN ME

The self in me
When confidence fades
Must look to the Lord,
His grace and mercy I claim.

The self in me
Can attack my heart,
Voices in my head
Take me down the wrong path.

The self in me
Can bring distress and grief,
In knowing God's mercy,
His love rescues me.

The self in me
Need never doubt,
I claim God's deliverance,
That's what Calvary was about.

The self in me
Can no longer make me sway,
His Holy Spirit changed me,
I'm guided by Him today.

The self in me
Has changed from long ago,
The Saviour taught me forgiveness
And now His love I show.

RISE ABOVE THESE DOUBTS

When confidence seems to fail,
Doubts start creeping in,
Turn to His Word,
You can remain strong in Him.

The Lord knows your troubles
And is there to help you through,
Trust in your faith,
His strength will come to you.

He will spur you on to joyfulness
Through His Spirit who cares for you,
He brings His healing and comfort
If you ask Him too.

Come into His presence,
Your needs He wants to know,
You can rise above these doubts
Because He loves you so.

In His Glory you have His light
That shines on precious you,
Rise above these doubts
He wants the best for you.

REST IN HIS LOVE

Rest in the Lord's love
When cares take their toll,
Leave them with the Saviour,
He is in control.

Take shelter in His arms
When shadows come near,
He will protect your fragile heart
Until they disappear.

Rest in His love
With trust and faith,
He will reward you so much
With His mercy and grace.

Rest in His love,
It is the only way,
Rest in His love,
Jesus came to save!

IN THE NAME OF JESUS...
PRAY FOR OTHERS...

"...Pray on every occasion, as the Spirit leads. For this reason keep alert and never give up; pray always for all God's people."

Ephesians 6 : 18

YOU KNOW AND YOU SEE

Lord, you know and You see
Everything we do,
You know our battles
And long to help us through.

There's so much heartache
That you know and see,
The downfall of man
Who You long to set free.

We grow in our faith
When we look to Thee,
We can ask for Your guidance
Which will change our inner needs.

With the help of Your Spirit
Who lives within,
He gives us the strength
And the courage to win.

Lord, you know and You see
And will take our misery,
You can turn it into good
When we trust and believe.

IN HIS NAME

We can't do the impossible,
That only God can do,
In His Name we can rise above
To solutions, that is true.

In His Name we can rise above
Challenges that find us,
We can have victory
When we use our faith and trust.

Pray in Jesus Name
And believe in your heart,
Ask for His help
So life's challenges can pass.

In His Name we can rise above
All things that come our way,
We can look to His light,
That will never fade.

Call on His Name,
Never doubt what He can do,
The impossible is possible
Because He truly loves you.

PASSAGE OF LIFE

The passage of life is strewn
With a myriad of events,
Some big and small,
Some too precious to forget.

In Christ we can overcome
The battles we face,
Through the passage of life
His hand we can take.

The believing heart has access
To the storehouse of God,
To restore and refresh us
With the needs we rely upon.

Shadows may cross our path
But the Lord's light is there,
A beam so blinding
That will lift any cares.

The passage of life brings questions
That only God knows the reason why,
Look to His mercy and grace
That is yours through the passage of life.

OPEN HEARTS

Open your heart to the Saviour
The One True God,
He took your sin forever
When He hung on Calvary's Cross.

He loves you endlessly,
No matter what you've done,
So, open your heart to the Saviour,
God's only precious Son.

He knows what you think
And He sees into your heart,
For His daily help
You only have to ask.

Be true to yourself
By confessing to God,
Open your heart to Jesus,
His ways you can lean upon.

You will have an awakening
Like nothing you've ever known,
Open your heart to the Saviour,
His precious Spirit you will own!

MATURITY IN FAITH

Maturity in faith brings refinement
By leaving life's challenges behind,
Memories once so real
Will fade with passing time.

Maturity alters the mould
We see with a different view,
Once we were cold and defiant,
But in the Spirit we are renewed.

Maturity in faith brings peace
As you slowly change your ways,
Respond to the Saviour today,
You will wear His Robe of Grace.

Your heart will open in His love
Like the clay in the potter's hands,
Press into the Saviour today,
You are part of His heavenly plan.

LIFETIME FRIENDS

Lifetime friends
Are a blessing indeed,
Chosen by the Saviour,
He knows just who we need.

He places them on our path,
They shine like the stars above,
We share each other's journey
Because we share the Saviour's love.

God sends lifetime friends,
Who we carry in our hearts,
So special and precious,
A blessing to impart.

Lifetime friends bring happiness,
They share our joys and fears,
They are brought by the Saviour
Because He holds us so dear.

PROVIDE ME LORD...
WITH ALL MY NEEDS...

"Christ's message in all its richness must live in your hearts. Teach and instruct one another with all wisdom. Sing psalms, hymns, and sacred songs; sing to God with thanksgiving in your hearts."

Colossians 3 : 16

YOU KNOW ME

You know me Lord,
What I think and say,
Help me to keep Your counsel
In my life every day.

You know me Lord
When a challenge comes,
Will I rise above it
Or will I succumb?

You know me Lord
When I'm happy or sad,
Help me to think good thoughts
Instead of the bad.

You know me Lord,
The choice is mine,
In my every day walk,
I can choose to shine.

Your love is so special
From Your divine heart,
You know me well Lord,
From my first day to the last.

You know me Lord,
You made every part of me,
I thank You for Your love
That gives me Eternity.

KINDLY DEEDS

The world holds no mercy
With its jealousy and greed,
Encouragement seems lost
For kindly deeds.

God sees into each heart,
His peace He will share,
You can be a powerhouse,
For you He truly cares.

He craves for kindly deeds
For us all to pass along,
Being a powerhouse,
In His light you belong.

The world needs kindly deeds,
In His Name we can supply,
We can help each other
If on Jesus we rely.

KEEP PEACE IN YOUR HEART

Keep peace in your heart,
No matter what comes your way,
Ask for the Saviour's help
Each and every day.

His Word is always there
To comfort you in need,
He longs for your attention
Because He is God's Holy Seed.

Keep peace in your heart,
The kind His Spirit sends,
When you confess Him "Lord",
Any cares He will amend.

Keep peace in your heart
Though challenges may rise,
Call on the Saviour,
Our glorious Shining Light.

Keep peace in your heart,
You are a powerhouse for God,
His Light shines forever
That you can pass along.

I'M WAITING ON YOU LORD

I'm waiting on You Lord
To direct my daily steps,
I need Your direction
For what comes next.

I'm waiting on You Lord
To show me a path
That opens before me,
You already know what I will ask.

I'm waiting on You Lord
Because You're my God,
My friend and my Saviour,
You, I can lean upon.

Yes, I'm waiting on You Lord,
My guide and my hope,
Trust and faith I have in You
The God I know.

I'M IN YOUR HANDS

I'm adoring You Lord,
I'm in Your hands,
My trust and faith
Only You understand.

I'm in Your hands Lord,
You created me,
Everything around me,
Your beauty I see.

Your hands so precious
They calmed the storm,
They were tied and pierced
To bring prophecy forth.

I'm in Your hands Lord,
They heal open wounds,
Your miracle healing balm
Pours out to soothe.

I revere You as my King,
Your will be done,
Through Your grace and mercy
From You the living Son.

I'm in Your hands Lord,
My heart I give to You,
Through Your Spirit I'm saved,
Refreshed, restored, renewed.

EVERYTHING IN ITS PLACE

Everything in its place
Timed perfectly by God,
A reason stands behind
Events that come along.

As revealed in His Word
"A time and place" we read,
Sometimes it takes a while
For these things to appear.

Our plans may not work
Because God's plans prevail,
But if we seek His counsel
We surely cannot fail.

Keeping an open heart
Will help us understand,
Everything in its place,
By God's Holy plan.

YOU, LORD...
ARE A BEACON IN MY LIFE...

"I have the strength to face all conditions by the power that Christ gives me."

Philippians 4 : 13

CONSENT TO HIS LOVE

He's waiting for you
To consent to His love,
By inviting Him into your heart
Where His Spirit will come.

He will never force Himself
Into your life,
He waits for your invitation
To shine His precious light.

He may use other people
To shine His light on you,
To prompt you with a message
That will encourage you.

His awakening is real
As it strikes your heart,
When you feel His Spirit coming
He will lift you out of the dark.

You will have the gift of Eternity,
He will be by your side,
Consent to His love
You shall wear the Crown of Life.

COME AS YOU ARE

Come as you are
To the Throne of God,
Rich or poor, strong or weak
That's where you belong.

He made you in His image
But unique in every way,
Each one He gave special gifts
To share along life's way.

He wants you just as you are
To give your heart to Him,
Come and be renewed
He wants you to welcome Him in.

He died on the Cross at Calvary
To pay for our sins,
He loves us so much,
Know pure joy within.

Come as you are,
He will show you victory
Over all the challenges of life,
He can set you free.

PATIENCE

Lay patience on my heart Lord
To wait for answered prayer,
In the Spirit's love
I am in Your care.

Lay patience on my heart Lord
When I'm reading Your Word,
Help me find the answers
For which I am in search.

Lay patience on my heart Lord
So humble I become,
Through the shadows and the valleys
I can overcome.

Lay patience on my heart Lord
To see Your heavenly smile,
As I continue on my journey,
Mile after mile.

CLEAR IT AWAY

Whatever is heavy
Let Jesus clear it away,
A problem laying on your heart,
Tell Him today!

Use your trust and faith,
You don't have to carry that load,
Let God clear it away
You are not alone.

Though challenges come along,
In faith your trust will grow,
Let God clear it away
For He truly knows.

Believe that you can overcome
With His help every day,
In faith you will receive
His strength, come what may.

Call on God today,
His mercy will spill over you,
Confide in Him this moment,
He surely wants you to!

CHALLENGES

In these challenging times
When the world is on her knees,
Mankind must come together
It's time to reflect on "Thee".

We can pray for His healing touch
And state our case to Him,
We can give our heart's desire,
There's a power greater within.

When challenges stand up
And shake our world upside down
Beyond our personal reckoning,
But God's love can still be found.

If we look around at His creation,
Rolling seas and setting sun,
We can look above the chaos
To the King of Glory's precious love.

God is still with us
He's never left your side,
Be sure He cares for you,
In Him you can confide.

BEFRIEND THE SAVIOUR

Don't fall short of happiness
That is pure and true,
When you befriend the Saviour
He will bring these joys to you.

He longs for you to have
A happy heart right now,
Let go of your hurts and fears,
He can show you how.

He patiently waits
For you to claim His love,
There's nothing He'd rather do
But come into your heart.

Befriend the Saviour
Daily into your life,
There's nothing He can't do,
To make everything right.

He adores you full score
And He only wants the best,
To fill your life with His supply,
Befriend Christ the unseen Guest!

YOU WILL GROW IN HIS LOVE

You will grow in His love
Through your faith and trust,
A power so overwhelming
Because He first loved us.

He taught us how to live,
To abide by His Word,
For freedom from doubt and fear,
Read His powerful Word.

You will grow in His love,
A love that knows no end,
It's full of power and strength
From His Spirit that He sends.

You will grow in His love,
Ask the Saviour how,
Such a precious gift,
Come as you are now!

You will grow in His love
Because The Spirit lives inside,
No finer way to live,
By grace you will abide.

BAPTISM OF HOLY LOVE

A baptism of Holy Love
Is when God comes close to you,
He reveals His Holy Spirit
Who makes you feel brand new.

No wonders can describe
His Spirit who He sends,
His gift when you believe
He is your eternal friend.

Through the Holy Spirit
God's love comes to stay,
He dwells in your heart
Where His grace can be displayed.

His baptism of Holy Love
Continues for the rest of your life,
God's Holy endowment,
Your pathway into His Light.

THE PRECIOUS NAZARENE

You are saved by His Name;
The precious Nazarene,
The Messiah born in Bethlehem
Would be God's Holy seed.

He was cared for so lovingly
By His earthly family,
Son of a carpenter,
He became a Nazarene.

The Spirit led Him to the desert
For forty days and nights,
Where He prepared for His Ministry
He emerged with power and might.

He chose His disciples
To make His message known,
He taught them parables
Because He loved them so.

They witnessed many things,
Some hard to believe,
When He appeared to them
Walking on the sea.

These powerful experiences
Shown by the Nazarene
Forever changed the Disciples,
Who were led to believe.

THE CHRISTIAN HEART

In the scheme of life
We make decisions and plans,
But the Christian heart
Should leave them in God's hands.

The Christian heart has good intentions
But sometimes loses sight
Of Jesus who goes ahead,
Who guides us in His light.

The Christian heart has a conscience,
It knows right from wrong,
Through the Holy Spirit
We are guided along.

All is not bright
When we disappoint ourselves,
But we can look to Jesus
To take His hand for help.

He knows our misgivings
But still loves us unconditionally,
He lives in the Christian heart
Because He gave us Calvary.

The Christian heart has victory
When it claims God's will,
We can be a power house for God
For His plan to be fulfilled.

TALK THROUGH YOUR HEART

Talk through your heart
For truth to be exposed,
A love no understanding
Will ever know.

Talk through your heart
For kindness to show,
Where the love of God
Through His Spirit will grow.

Talk through your heart
He will spread gentleness to give,
A knowing you will feel
He will change the way you live.

Yes, talk through your heart,
His Spirit lives there,
His grace and mercy will be yours
That you will want to share.

STAY CONNECTED

Stay connected to God
No matter your circumstance,
Remember He planned your life
And moulded you with His hands.

He gave us freedom of choice
To choose our way in life,
Listen for His voice
So His way you will find.

He waits for your invitation
To shine His light on you,
Then you will be connected
To receive His grace and truth.

Stay connected to God
To put your fears to rest,
Left in His hands,
Our heavenly Father knows what's best.

Stay connected to God,
Be saved by His Holy Spirit,
Share your prayers with Him,
Be sure He will receive them.

PART THREE

"Remember how great is God's power;
he is the greatest teacher of all."

Job 36 : 22

THERE'S POWER...
IN YOUR WORD LORD...

"Your word is a lamp to guide me
and a light for my path."

Psalm 119 : 105

THE ME I THOUGHT I KNEW

There comes a time in life
When you look at yourself,
Something's not quite right
So you turn to God for help.

The me I thought I knew
Thinks "I'd never do that"
But I let Jesus down
From words I can't take back.

He wants us every day
To look to Him for strength,
He is our eternal Counsellor
For every challenge we meet.

Sometimes we fall short
And disappoint ourselves,
God still loves us all,
He knows us so well.

The me I thought I knew
Is covered by His grace,
I repent in heartfelt prayer
As I seek His face.

The me I thought I knew
Can rise to victory,
His Spirit lives within,
Because of Calvary.

HIS LOVE WILL PREVAIL

His love will prevail
In all you do,
Accept Him into your heart,
His love will own you.

His Spirit will thrill you
Like nothing before,
His Spirit will love you
It's you He adores.

A true revelation
When you see His face,
A transformation in your heart
Will surely take place.

His love will prevail,
Read His Word and learn
His eternal ways,
Because you, He came to serve.

His love will prevail
Because He is power and majesty,
His love will prevail,
He will come in victory.

No lightning storm can outshine
The glory of His Light,
His love will prevail
With supremacy and might.

REACHING INTO ETERNITY

I'm reaching into Eternity Lord
From the love You provide,
I'm reaching into Eternity
Because Your love I just can't hide.

My faith and trust reveal
Your power on earth,
I can reach into Eternity
Because You came to serve.

I love to focus on You
The Lord of my life,
I'm reaching into Eternity
Because You are my shining light.

Every day of my life
Your Spirit brings You close
I feel so blessed Lord
To know You, my glorious Heavenly Host.

The power of Your Name Lord
Reaches into my soul,
I can reach into Eternity
Because You have made me whole.

PROCLAIM YOUR TRUST AND FAITH

Proclaim your trust and faith
In the Saviour above,
Take every care to Him,
His answer will come.

Go quietly in your witness
Of His precious love,
And the sacrifice He made
For our eternal home above.

Proclaim your trust and faith
Because in Him you believe,
That He paid the price for all
So a crown we could receive.

Proclaim your trust and faith
In the Holy Trinity,
Father, Son and Holy Spirit,
They love you endlessly.

PLACE PRAYERS IN HIS HANDS

Place prayers in His hands
For all your concerns,
Daily talk to Jesus
For you He yearns.

Thank Him for your blessings
Whether large or small,
He wants to share your journey
And help you with it all.

Take your heart felt cares
And your journey that you plan,
Place these prayers
In His precious hands.

Bring them all to His Altar
Where He waits for you,
Place your prayers in His hands
So He can help you through.

MY REAL HOME

My real home Lord
Is made by You,
This world I know
But I'm only passing through.

My real home dwells
In the heavens above
Where You abide
In Your world full of love.

My real home for now
I cannot really grasp,
The wonders of Heaven
Beyond what I can ask.

My real home is waiting
In Your glorious realm above,
In ecstasy and awe
Is the wonder of Your love.

My real home is vast
Within Heaven's lights,
It lies waiting in Eternity
Angels singing with delight.

In majesty and wonder
I will see Him on His Throne,
His glory will be revealed
In my real home.

KEEP YOUR HEART SOFT…
WITH GOD'S LOVE…

"Let us try to know the Lord. He will come to us as surely as the spring rains fall upon the earth."

Hosea 6 : 3

RHAPSODY OF LOVE

Rhapsody of love
Brought by the Lord Himself,
Moments of victory I feel,
Pure joy untold is felt.

Moments of completeness
Eventually do arrive,
A lengthy wait
In the Saviour's time.

The blessings He pours out
When I yield to His love,
Moments so glorious
I receive from above.

Rhapsody of love
No other can supply,
The Holy Trinity,
On them I do rely.

Rhapsody of love
Shines like the stars above,
His Spirit will live forever
In my heart for years to come!

REST IN HIS SPIRIT

When a challenge stands before you,
Rest in the Spirit's love,
He's the Comforter, Guide and Healer,
Sent by God above.

He lives within you always
To build your trust and faith,
When a challenge stands before you
He will come with mercy and grace.

Nothing can stand against Him,
No course can bar the way,
His Spirit will raise you up
So you can overcome today.

So when a challenge stands before you,
Give it to God today
Rest in the Spirit's love
You; He came to save!

AWAKENING

When I call to You Lord
An awakening comes to me,
A realization of who You are
Through Your winds of peace.

I sense Your majesty,
A calm flows over me,
Your Spirit brings Your love
In true tranquility.

An awakening of Your presence
Is what I truly see,
The gift of Your love
From You I have received.

An awakening of Your presence Lord,
Is pure reality,
The wonder of Your love Lord,
The blessed Trinity.

THE YOU I LOVE

Mankind is Your passion Lord
Who you love more than words can say,
We are never out of Your reach
As you guide us day by day.

You wait for my invitation
To call You into my heart,
The You I love, my Saviour,
Our union will never part.

The You I love, precious Jesus,
My Redeemer and my God,
Who came to save me long ago,
You gave Your body and Your blood.

The You I love, is love,
No sin in You is seen,
Your sacrifice so faithful,
You took the Cross for me.

The You I love, is eternal,
Forever You will be,
Creator, Healer and Prince,
One of the Holy Trinity.

The You I love, will never pass away,
Your Words will echo in ageless time,
Your wonder, awe and majesty
Will be forever mine!

YOU KNOW US WELL

You know us well Lord,
More than we know ourselves,
You see into our hearts
But You say "all is well".

You know our selfishness
And how and why we act,
But in You we can overcome
Because there's nothing we will lack.

In You we can have
A more forgiving heart,
We can see differently
Through Your Spirit if we ask.

You know us well Lord
But we must commit to Your ways,
We can have a heart like Yours
If we listen to what You say.

You know us well Lord
But You love us just the same,
You took our sin to Calvary
We are saved by Your Name.

STAND FIRM IN HIS LOVE

Use your trust and faith
To stand firm in His love,
When a challenge comes your way
Give it to God above.

Stand firm in His love
When fear and doubt flood your mind,
You need not worry,
Ask for His blessing every time.

You can have victory
If you stand firm in His love,
Open your heart to His will,
His answer will surely come.

Stand firm in His love
In every facet of life,
There's nothing He cannot do,
He will make your world so bright.

PART FOUR

"So Judas went to the garden taking with him a group of Roman soldiers, and some temple guards sent by the chief priests and the Pharisees; they were armed and carried lanterns and torches. Jesus knew everything that was going to happen to him, so he stepped forward and asked them "Who is it you are looking for?" "Jesus of Nazareth," they answered. "I am he," he said."…

John 18 : 3 - 5

BE A POWERHOUSE FOR GOD

HE SUFFERED...
SO WE COULD LIVE...

"It was about twelve o'clock when the sun stopped shining and darkness covered the whole country until three o'clock; and the curtain hanging in the Temple was torn in two. Jesus cried out in a loud voice, "Father! In your hands I place my spirit!" He said this and died.

Luke 23 : 44 - 46

CALVARY'S NAZARENE

A revelation to His chosen twelve,
He called them one by one,
They witnessed miracles and healing
From God's only Son.

When He was lifted up
On the hill at Calvary,
They feared for their lives
Because of the Nazarene.

God raised Him to life,
There was now an empty Tomb,
Then He appeared to the eleven
In a locked room.

Any doubt was gone forever,
They saw His hands and side
Wounded by the nails,
Their belief they couldn't hide.

An awakening yet to come
He would meet them privately,
The Blessing from above
The Holy Spirit to receive.

Now full of His Spirit
To proclaim what they had seen,
Eternal life for all
Who believed in Calvary's Nazarene.`

BE AN EASTER LILY

Be an Easter Lily
All through the year,
Though you have weathered
Personal joy and tears.

Be an Easter Lily
Full of beauty and grace,
Stand firm in the Saviour's love
With trust and faith.

Though they only flower once a year,
Such a humble time,
The Saviour was lifted up
For the sake of mankind.

Our sin was nailed
With Him on the Cross,
He paid the price of redemption
But to us, no cost!

Be an Easter Lily,
Stand tall to wear His Name,
He's the foundation you can depend on,
His love will never change.

IN PASSION AND POWER

Through His passion and power
The Saviour took the Cross,
The passion of His love
We could never pay the cost.

Each soul is precious,
A heart to heal,
His hands and feet wounded
As Scripture revealed.

By His Father's power
He rose from the grave,
Victorious over death
By His Blood we are saved.

It was His passion and power
That led Him to the Cross,
Because of His Resurrection
We will never be lost.

Through His passion and power
He rose to victory,
For us He lives
In our home called Eternity!

BE A POWERHOUSE FOR GOD

JESUS HAS RISEN...
EVERLASTING GLORY AND MAJESTY...

"He has been raised to the right side of God,
his Father, and has received from him the
Holy Spirit, as he had promised."...

Acts 2 : 33

HOLY WEEK

Holy Week touches my soul
And stirs it to the depths,
A feeling so overwhelming
That I just can't comprehend.

In faith I accept
His sacrifice for me,
A love like no other
Drove Him to Calvary.

A power so great
Raised Him to life,
He left the tomb forever
And rose in glorious Light.

Holy Week consecrates
The Will of God,
Through His precious Son
Who was nailed to the Cross.

Holy Week is a time
To reflect and respond
Where my life is going,
Is it earth's highway or the Cross?

Holy Week the gateway
Of the entrance to His Throne,
Through His grace and mercy
He will make me His own.

REUNION

Reunion so special,
The stone was rolled away,
The Saviour was raised,
It was Easter Day.

Reunion with the Father
After the darkness of Calvary,
Scriptures prophesied,
He will rise in victory.

The Father gave Him great glory
By raising Him to life,
A miracle only by God
Overturning darkness to Light.

A reunion so special,
Father God and Holy Son,
Returning to the Throne,
The battle over death is won.

Now in Heaven's splendour
Father and Son sit side by side,
Majestic wonder all around,
Forever they will abide.

Their reunion now eternal
In Heaven they abide,
The darkness of Calvary
Gives way to Paradise.

MARY GAVE BIRTH...
ON THE HOLIEST OF NIGHTS...

"The angel said to her, "Don't be afraid, Mary; God has been gracious to you. You will become pregnant and give birth to a son, and you will name him Jesus. He will be great and will be called the Son of the Most High God."...

Luke 1 : 30 - 32

HER NAME WAS MARY

A young girl she was
Chosen by God,
To bear His Holy Son
Who the world would lean upon.

Her name was Mary,
A quiet and gentle soul,
Obedient to her Heavenly Father,
His Only Son she would hold.

Conceived by the Holy Spirit
She would carry the Holy Child,
She gave birth in the Stable
On a deep night, so quiet.

He was born that Holy Night
Joseph was by her side,
Angels stepped down from Heaven
With a message from on high.

She wrapped Him in swaddling clothes,
Held Him close to her heart,
In a dimly lit Stable
God's will had come to pass!

Mother of the Holy Christ Child,
Mary, was her name,
A humble faithful servant,
Blessed, she remains.

HALLELUJAH IN THE HIGHEST

Hallelujah in the highest,
Jesus Christ is born
On the Holiest of nights,
Shepherds came to adore.

The blazing Star lit the sky
In divine majesty,
Shrouding the Holy family,
Angels sing in harmony.

Heavenly Hosts proclaim
The arrival of the Messiah King,
Humbly in the stable
Eternal life He brings.

Hallelujah in the highest,
The Saviour has arrived,
Wrapped in swaddling clothes,
This Holy, Holy night.

Hallelujah in the highest,
Eternal joy has come
To save the world from sin,
God's precious only Son.

IN THE MANGER HE LAY

In the Manger He lay,
God's precious Holy Son,
Wrapped in swaddling clothes,
Salvation has come.

No room in The Inn
On that Holy Night,
A Stable was the place
For the Saviour to arrive.

Angels and shepherds proclaimed
Joy has come to the world,
They bowed down to worship Him,
The Son of God; they beheld.

What wonder and awe
Filled the Stable that night,
The lamb and the calf
Knew the Holy Christ.

In the Manger He lay,
The everlasting Lord,
The Saviour of the world,
He, we must adore.

NO GIFTS UNDER THE TREE

We decorate Christmas trees
With coloured lights and gifts beneath,
The Spirit of Christmas we share
But for many no joy to receive.

Some still haven't heard
How the Saviour was born that Holy Night,
How angels sang with great joy
Of His birth that Christmas Night.

Holy angels rejoiced in Heaven,
The Saviour of the world has arrived,
Through Mary, God sent His Son,
She gave birth that Holy Night.

You are not alone
If there are no gifts under the tree,
You can still find solace in Jesus,
He was born to set you free.

He is the Lord Jesus Christ,
The greatest gift to behold,
Born lowly in a stable,
Down through the ages His story is told.

You can have joy this Christmas,
Open His Word to read how,
You can worship and adore Him
Where you are right now!

ALSO BY CLAIRE GROSE

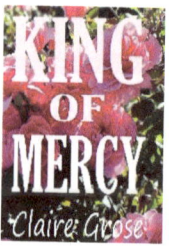
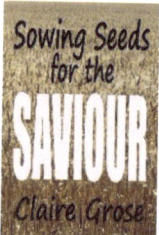
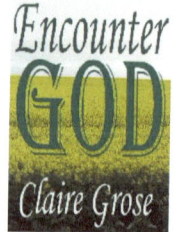

ABOUT THE AUTHOR

Claire worked as a Government Public Servant in the Lands Department, Adelaide, South Australia until she married and became a mother of two boys.

She later returned to the work force during which time she gained a "Living Hope" Phone Counselling certificate which influenced her need to help others.

Through this and personal experience she found herself inspired by God's love to put pen to paper.

PHOTO CREDITS

COVER PHOTO: Veale Gardens; Adelaide – Claire Grose

Page 2: Yellow Rose; S.A. – Claire Grose
Page 12: Spring Garden; S.A. – Michael and Andrea
Page 24: Spring Blossoms; S.A. – Claire Grose
Page 31: Crepe Myrtle; Vic. – Jette and Pete
Page 39: Lilac Tree flowers; S.A. – Lindsay
Page 47: Rose Garden; Vic. – Jette and Pete
Page 55: Flower Bouquet; S.A. – Claire Grose
Page 70: Windchimes; Qld – Carol and Dennis
Page 78: Salvia plant; Qld. – Claire Grose
Page 87: Salisbury Uniting Church Cross; S.A. – Claire Grose
Page 92: Salisbury Uniting Church Cross; S.A. – Claire Grose
Page 96: Salisbury Uniting Church Cross; S.A. – Claire Grose

BE A POWERHOUSE FOR GOD

www.ingramcontent.com/pod-product-compliance
Lightning Source LLC
Chambersburg PA
CBHW042043290426
44109CB00001B/12